SCIENCE ENCYCLOPEDIA
GENERAL SCIENCE

An imprint of Om Books International

Contents

Broad Branches of Science	4
History of Science	6
Science Today	8
Importance of Science	10
Atoms	12
Molecules	13
Electrons	14
Elements	15
Chemical Bonds	16
The Periodic Table	18
History of the Periodic Table	20
Periodic Trends	21
Valency	22
Definition of Matter	24
Phases of Matter and Phase Diagram	25
States of Matter	26
Properties of Matter	28
Greenhouse Effect and Greenhouse Gases	30
Arresting Global Warming	31

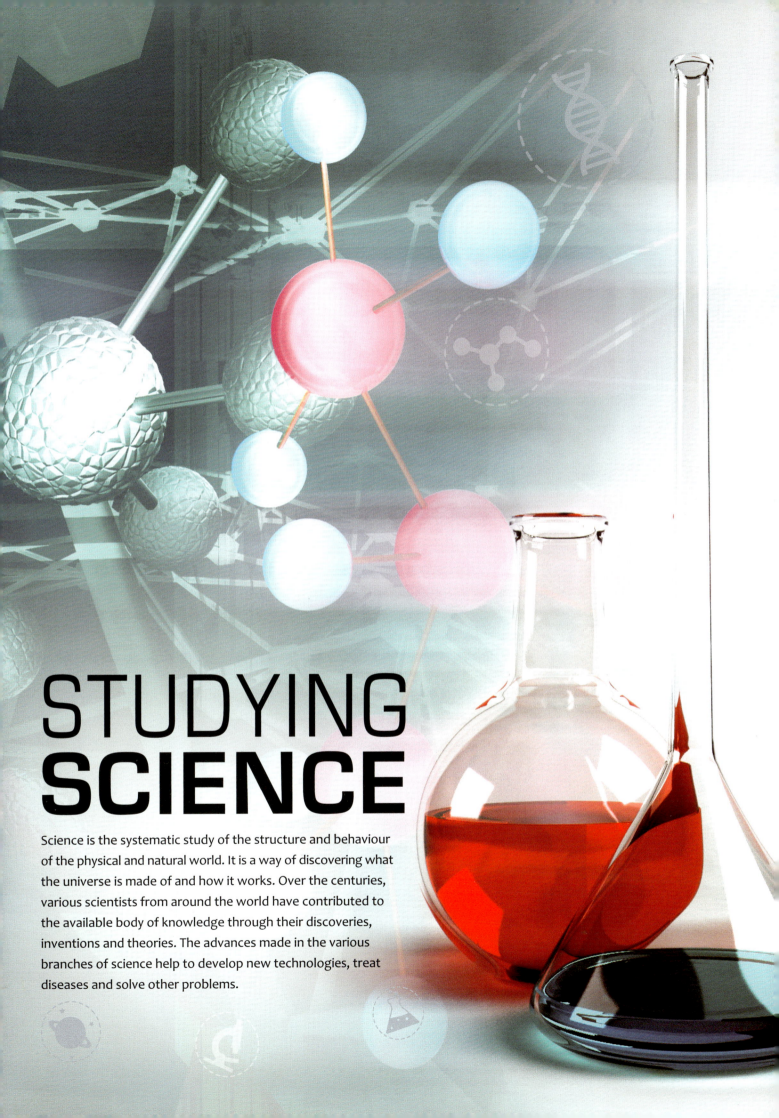

STUDYING SCIENCE

Science is the systematic study of the structure and behaviour of the physical and natural world. It is a way of discovering what the universe is made of and how it works. Over the centuries, various scientists from around the world have contributed to the available body of knowledge through their discoveries, inventions and theories. The advances made in the various branches of science help to develop new technologies, treat diseases and solve other problems.

SCIENCE ENCYCLOPEDIA

Broad Branches of Science

The branches of science are broadly divided into four categories: chemical, physical, life and mathematical. These four categories constitute the fundamental sciences, which form the basis of interdisciplinary and applied sciences, such as engineering and medicine.

Chemical science

Chemical science, also known as chemistry, is defined as the study of matter and its interactions with other matter and energy. Everything involves chemistry as all matter is made up of atoms. Even the human body is made up of various chemical elements and its different activities involve chemical processes.

Central science

Chemistry acts like a crossroad for other branches of science as many of its branches have common features with other sciences, like physics. So, it is considered as the "central science". Scientists who study chemistry are called chemists.

Physical science

Physical science, also known as physics, is one of the major branches of science that explains the measure of different physical quantities like speed, distance, energy, motion, etc., which play a vital role in daily human life.

All about the math

Physical science relies heavily on mathematics. Models and theories in physics are articulated using mathematical equations. Although physics uses mathematics to explain the material world, mathematics generally deals with abstract concepts. These two fields significantly overlap each other in an area known as mathematical physics.

Studying chemicals and their reactions.

Pendulum showing perpetual motion.

Mathematical science

The combined study of mathematics and science is called mathematical science. Statistics, for example, is mathematical in nature, but is evolved through scientific observation. Other fields that are sometimes considered as mathematical sciences include computer science, computational science, population genetics, operations research, cryptology, econometrics, theoretical physics and actuarial science. Innovations in technology could not have been possible without mathematical science.

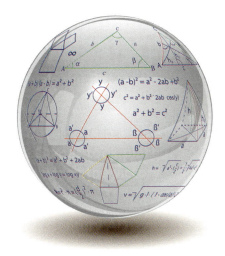

The spectrum of mathematical science.

Life science

Life science is the study of living organisms. It describes the characteristics, classification and behaviour of organisms, how species came into existence and the interactions that they have with each other and the environment. It has many sub-branches that focus on a specific type of life form, for example, zoology is the study of animals, botany is the study of plants, etc.

Life science plays an important role in the agriculture, medicine and food science industries. Thus, it helps to improve the standard of human life. Life science is very closely related to chemical science.

Exploring different life forms.

GENERAL SCIENCE

These fields also fall under the science category!

1. **Linguistics** is the scientific study of language. A person who studies languages is called a linguist. Linguists study every aspect of human language, ranging from translating cuneiform tablets to tracking tweets to attempting to isolate and analyse the faces that children make when they are lying.

2. **Criminology** is the scientific study of crime. It involves studying the causes of crimes, responses by law enforcement agencies and crime prevention methods. It is a sub-group of sociology, which is the scientific study of social behaviour. Many fields of study are used in the field of criminology, which include biology, statistics, psychology, psychiatry, economics and anthropology. A person studying such a field is called a criminologist.

3. **Planetary geology**, also known as **astrogeology**, involves the study of the geology of celestial bodies, such as planets and their moons, asteroids, comets and meteorites. It mainly deals with determining the internal structure of terrestrial planets and also examines planetary volcanism. The structures of giant planets and their moons are also studied along with minor bodies of the solar system, such as asteroids, the Kuiper Belt and comets.

SCIENCE ENCYCLOPEDIA

History of Science

Before science was recognised as a distinct field and various discoveries were made, people attributed various scientific phenomena to magic! It took a while to understand the reasoning behind these occurrences. Different civilisations around the world devised their own theories and made significant contributions to the field of science. Let us look at some of their achievements.

During the reign of Nebuchadnezzar, priests calculated the paths of planets and plotted the orbits of the Sun and the moon.

Babylonian science

Babylonians used a numeral system with 60 as its base. This allowed them to divide circles into 360 degrees. They were remarkably talented in astronomy, where magic, mysticism, astrology and divination were the main drivers. They believed that the movement of celestial bodies predicted terrestrial events. They kept complete lists of eclipses and by 700 BCE, it was known that solar eclipses only occurred during new moons and lunar eclipses during full moons.

Egyptian science

Despite their belief in superstitions, Egyptian priests encouraged the development of many scientific disciplines, especially astronomy and mathematics. The Rhind Mathematical Papyrus is an ancient mathematical treatise, dating back to around 1650 BCE. It explains how to calculate the area of a field, the capacity of a barn and it also deals with algebraic equations of the first degree. The Egyptians were also the first to calculate the value of "pi" as 22/7 (3.14).

The construction of the pyramids and other monuments would have been impossible without significant mathematical knowledge.

GENERAL SCIENCE

Indian science

The Vedas, a body of texts composed between 1500 and 1000 BCE in India, explained some aspects of astronomical science. They divided the year into 12 lunar months, sometimes adding another month to adjust with the solar year. Many ceremonies and sacrificial rites in ancient India were regulated by the position of the moon the Sun and other astronomical events.

Development of geometry

The fundamentals of geometry can be traced back to the rigid religious rules followed for the construction of sacrifice altars in India. One of Ancient India's greatest achievements however, was the study of arithmetic. This included the development of numbers and decimals, still in use, today, across the world. Even the 'Arabic numbers' were first observed on rock edicts from the Mauryan period of Emperor Ashoka, over 1000 years before they appeared in Arabic literature.

Greek science

Unlike other parts of the world where science was strongly connected with religion, Greek scientific thought had a stronger connection with philosophy. The Greek scientific spirit had a more secular approach and was able to replace the notion of supernatural explanation with the concept of a universe that is governed by the laws of nature. According to Greek tradition, credit goes to Thales of Miletus, who lived somewhere in 600 BCE, for proposing that natural laws best explain the world.

Influence of Egyptian math

The influence of Egyptian mathematics was first seen in Greece, back in the 26th Dynasty (c. 685–525 BCE), when Egyptian ports began trading with the Greeks. Babylonian astronomy came with the conquest of Mesopotamia and Asia Minor by Alexander.

The Sun is one of the many gods that Indians worship. This is why a lot of occasions and events are planned based on its position in the solar system.

Chinese science

In ancient China, government officials were concerned with areas of scientific progress. Astronomy and mathematics interested the court astronomers who understood the importance of the calendar and the happenings in the sky. From the time of Confucius, Chinese astronomers were known to have successfully recorded eclipses. The need to measure land led to the development of geometry. Ancient Indians gave us the knowledge of Algebra. The Ancient Chinese have also been credited with the discovery of the compass, gunpowder and wood and paper printing. However, the period between the Han dynasty and the fall of the Manchu dynasty (1912 CE) saw negligible progress in the industrial development of China.

FUN FACT

Every time an eclipse occurred, the Vikings assumed that the Sun and the moon were being chased by two wolves, Skoll and Hati. When either of the wolves successfully caught their prey, it would result in an eclipse.

Paper was one of China's many inventions.

SCIENCE ENCYCLOPEDIA

Science Today

Science has come a long way in the last 150 years. Gregor Mendel began investigating the sphere of plant genetics in the 1800s. Around 150 years later, modern plant genetics laboratories employed the latest DNA sequencing techniques. J.J. Thomson discovered a new particle of matter—the electron—at the turn of the century using vacuum tubes, magnets and simple wiring. Today, 100 years later, scientists searching for particles like the Higgs boson are using a supercollider—a 27-km-long machine and generating data analysed by the most powerful supercomputer. Let us explore the pathbreaking progress that science has made in the last few decades.

Human embryonic stem cells

Human embryonic stem cells can alter themselves into any tissue in the body. In 1998, scientists isolated the first human embryonic stem cells, which raised hopes for new cell-based therapies. However, as human embryos are destroyed during the process of cell extraction, the process raised ethical concerns. In 2007, two teams of researchers used genetic modification to transform ordinary skin cells into cells that appear to function like embryonic stem cells. The use of these reprogrammed cells, known as induced pluripotent stem (IPS) cells, might resolve the ethical concerns.

Contribution of life science

The era of modern science is majorly marked by research in the field of life science, which has significantly contributed to improving human life, in the areas of food, health and other areas of industry. The advances in life sciences have especially helped in the development of effective methods of diagnosis, treatment and prevention of several diseases.

The human embryonic cell.

Advances in technology have led to several pathbreaking discoveries.

8

GENERAL SCIENCE

FUN FACT
In 1989, using an atomic force microscope, IBM engineer Don Eigler became the first person to move and control a single atom.

Century of science

The rapid progress in science and technology during the late nineteenth and early twentieth centuries gave birth to the electrical and chemical industry, and led to the invention of automobiles and aeroplanes. All these developments and inventions resulted in economic advancement. Therefore, the twentieth century is called the "century of science".

Artificial intelligence

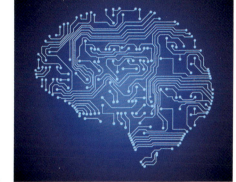

Human brain as an engineering processing machine signifying artificial intelligence.

Artificial intelligence (AI) is based on the thought that the process of human thinking can be mechanised. During the 1940s and 50s, scientists from different disciplines started thinking about the possibility of creating an artificial brain. AI research began in 1956; one of its goals was to make computers communicate in languages like English. During the late 70s, despite difficulties like financial setbacks and a negative public perception of AI, new ideas were explored in logic programming, commonsense reasoning and other similar areas.

Nanotechnology

Nanotechnology involves working with any substance on the atomic or molecular scale. National Nanotechnology Initiative defines it as, "the understanding and control of matter at dimensions between approximately one and 100 nanometres". At the nano (10^{-9} mm) level, the material properties change drastically, which can be used to develop many products and processes. Nanotechnology can create many new materials and devices in the fields of medicine, electronics, biomaterials, energy producing materials, etc.

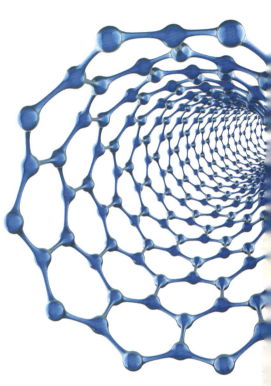

Nanotechnology is the study and application of very small things and can be used across all other science fields.

Neural network

Neural network refers to a computer modelled system that closely resembles the human brain and nervous system. During the 1940s, McCulloch and Pitts developed the first working neural model. Artificial neural networks are processing devices whose function is similar to that of the human neuronal system. They are widely used in biomedical research. They also have applications in the fields of diagnostics, robotics, business and medicine, where pattern recognition is required. In some specific areas, neural models achieve human-like performance over the more traditional AI techniques.

Neural networks are generally presented as systems of interconnected neurons.

SCIENCE ENCYCLOPEDIA

Importance of Science

Today, we are living in a world that is governed by science. The present era is that of science and technology. Science emerged as a result of our curiosity. It is just a means of searching for answers for the many questions that we have.

Life of ease

Science has made a significant difference to humankind. Today, we are living a comfortable life with many convenient technologies because of advancements made in the various fields of science. From the time we wake up to the time we go to bed, we come across many scientific inventions that have changed the way we live.

Body of knowledge

Science is a system of knowledge that is concerned with the physical world. It involves the pursuit of knowledge, covering general truths or operations of the fundamental laws of nature. However, it is far from a perfect instrument of knowledge. Formulation of hypothesis and use of various scientific formulas and methods are the major ways to add to the body of knowledge. Science also deals with reasoning, which is used to arrive at conclusions.

Philosophy of science

"Philosophy of science" is the branch of philosophy that deals with the study of science. It is primarily the motivation behind various approaches of science. A general philosophy of science aims to describe and understand how science works within a wide range of sciences. Even a basic understanding would enhance the knowledge of scientists working in that area.

Important inventions and changes

Electricity is one of the greatest inventions of science. Because of electricity, we no longer have dark days. Electricity has made it possible to stay cool during the hot summers and stay warm during the cold winters.

Further, advances in healthcare have improved the quality of human life. They have also helped decrease the mortality rate to a great extent and thus increase the longevity of human life.

Other inventions

Today, science has made the impossible possible. It has made survival easier than it was 100 years ago. Advancements made in the fields of science and technology have enabled us to be in touch with our near and dear ones. We have reached the moon and Mars due to these advances. Television, telephone, air conditioner, mobile, refrigerator and the internet are some of the inventions that we use in our everyday lives. Today, satellite systems are so advanced that they can warn us about upcoming natural calamities.

A modern racing wheelchair.

BUILDING BLOCKS

Molecules — the main structures that are involved in chemistry — are the building blocks of all the materials around us. Atoms are the basic constituents of molecules. A typical molecule may contain a few, a hundred or even a million atoms.

A molecule of table salt (NaCl) contains two atoms, that is, one atom of sodium (Na) and one atom of chlorine (Cl); a molecule of water (H_2O) contains two atoms of hydrogen and one atom of oxygen; a molecule of table sugar ($C_{12}H_{22}O_{11}$) contains 12 atoms of carbon, 11 atoms of oxygen and 22 atoms of hydrogen in a fixed arrangement.

SCIENCE ENCYCLOPEDIA

Atoms

Atoms are considered to be the basic constituent of any element or material. Therefore, knowledge of the structure of an atom is very crucial for understanding the properties of elements. An atom comprises a nucleus that is made up of protons and neutrons and surrounded by electrons. But how many electrons, protons and neutrons are present in an atom?

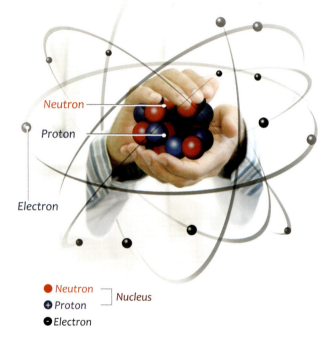

Structure of atom with respect to the position of electrons, neutrons and protons.

Construction of an atom

Atoms are composed of two regions: the nucleus and the electron cloud. The nucleus is the centre of the atom and it contains the major mass of the atom. The region around the nucleus where electrons are found occupies most of the space in the atom and is termed as an electron cloud. Protons and neutrons are found in the nucleus. The number of protons in the atom is the atomic number. The protons and neutrons are collectively called "nucleons" (protons + neutrons = nucleons). Protons have a positive charge (+1), electrons have a negative charge (–1), while neutrons are neutral (having no charge). Atomic mass is the total number of protons and neutrons in the nucleus. Atomic number is the number of protons in the nucleus of an atom, which is characteristic of a chemical element and determines its place in the periodic table.

Magic numbers in physics

Neutron to proton (n/p) ratio is defined as the ratio of the number of neutrons to the number of protons. The stability of the nucleus depends upon various factors including the n/p ratio. If the ratio is less than 1:1 or greater than 1.5:1, then the nucleus is considered to be highly unstable. To find the n/p ratio, find the number of neutrons by subtracting the number of protons from the atomic mass and divide by the number of electrons (which is the same as the atomic mass). The ratio generally increases with an increase in atomic number due to an increase in the repulsive force between the electrons and protons. Maria Goeppert-Mayer and other physicists proposed the concept of magic numbers, which give us the arrangement of nucleons inside an atomic nucleus. Magic numbers also determine the structural stability of an atom. The most recognised magic numbers are 2, 8, 20, 28, 50, 82 and 126.

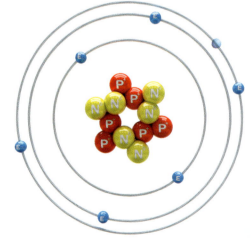

A schematic representation of an atom. Neutral atoms possess equal number of electrons and protons; however, they may possess varying numbers of neutrons.

Molecules

A molecule is a neutral component that is composed of two or more atoms of different elements that form a chemical bond. If we think of atoms as letters, then molecules are the words that the letters form. Thus, atoms are the building blocks of a molecule. A molecule can have a few or a hundred or more atoms.

Molecule of sodium chloride.

Elements like oxygen are unstable in their atomic state and so they react with another atom of their own to create an oxygen molecule (O_2). However, when reacting with hydrogen to create water, one atom of oxygen (O) reacts with two atoms of hydrogen (H_2) to form a water molecule (H_2O).

Dissimilarities from ions

Ions are atoms or molecules with a net electric charge due to the loss or gain of electrons. Molecules differ from ions as they don't have an electric charge. A molecule may have different complexes of atoms connected by covalent bonds (bonds formed by sharing electron pairs).

Crystals of molecules

Different molecules combine to form different substances, such as the components of the atmosphere. The minerals that comprise earth's core are composed of molecules of different elements. Usually, molecules of various elements form ionic bonds, thus combining to form compounds of various crystalline salts. When two molecules that differ in structure and electronic configuration form a compound, it results in a three-dimensional crystal, such as diamond.

Scientist conducting research on molecules.

Haphazard arrangement of molecules

In substances such as glass, the molecules may be held together in a manner that cannot be defined with regularity. However, every separate unit can be considered a crystal. Such bonds are covalent, which are not as strong as ionic or electrovalent bonds (bonds formed by transfer of electrons). Glass is composed of a combination of similar molecules.

Formation of three-dimensional crystal.

SCIENCE ENCYCLOPEDIA

Electrons

Atoms are composed of three subatomic particles called electrons, protons and neutrons. Among them, electrons are the smallest and are found in shells or orbits that surround an atom's nucleus. The motion of electrons in the electron cloud is similar to the motion of the planets around the Sun.

Information about electrons

Symbol: e^- or β^-

Discovered by: J. J. Thomson (1897)

Mass: 9.109×10^{-31} kg

Electric charge: -1.602×10^{-19} coulomb (C)

Plaque commemorating J. J. Thomson's discovery of the electron outside the old Cavendish Laboratory in Cambridge, UK

A beam of electrons deflected in a circle by a magnetic field.

Mass and location of electrons

Electrons possess minuscule mass, such that they exhibit properties of both particles and waves. It is impossible to learn the precise locations of electrons within a molecule. Despite such a limitation, there are regions around an atom where electrons have a high probability of being found. These regions are atomic orbits.

Charge of a body depends on the electron

When a body does not have the sufficient number of electrons that are required to balance the positive charge of the nuclei, then that body will not remain neutral. Instead, it will have an electric charge. The body is termed as negatively charged if it has more than the required number of electrons to balance it. Similarly, the body is termed as positively charged if it has less than the number of electrons that are required to balance the positive charge of the nucleus. Independent electrons that are not bound to an atom's nucleus and move in a vacuum are known as free electrons.

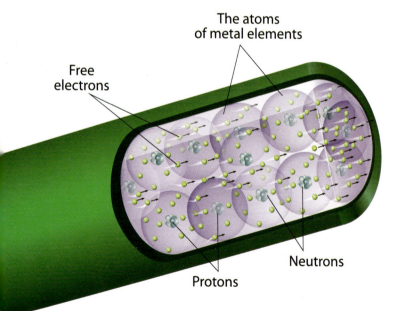

Electric current is the flow of electrons. In electric circuits, this charge is carried by moving electrons in a wire. A conductive metal contains free electrons, originating in conduction electrons.

Elements

An element is a pure substance that consists of only one type of atom and is distinguished by its atomic number. Each element in the periodic table has been classified as per its atomic number. Thus, before exploring an element, we should know what is meant by an atomic number.

Atomic number

The atomic number of an element is defined as the total number of protons present within the nucleus of an atom of that element. It is conventionally denoted by the symbol Z. Therefore, atomic number (Z) is equal to the number of protons in the atom. For example, one atom of carbon contains six protons; thus, the atomic number of carbon is six. Every element has a unique atomic number. The modern periodic table has been arranged by placing the elements according to their atomic numbers because no two elements share the same atomic number. Elements are broadly divided into three groups: metals, metalloids and non-metals.

Russian chemist Dmitri Mendeleev created a periodic table of the elements that ordered them numerically by atomic weight.

Mass number

Mass number is defined as the total number of protons and neutrons present within the nucleus of an atom. The mass number of an atom is conventionally denoted by the symbol A. Therefore, mass number (A) = number of protons + number of neutrons.

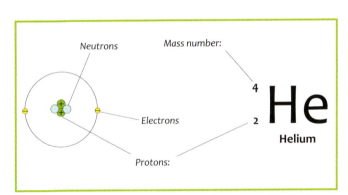

Atomic and mass number depiction.

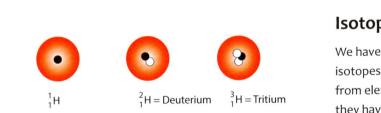

Isotopes

We have heard a lot about C-13, C-14 isotopes as well as the isotopes of uranium. What are isotopes? Are they different from elements? Isotopes are the variants of an element, as they have the same atomic number (Z) but have different atomic masses because they possess a different number of neutrons in their nuclei. Neutral atoms possess an equal number of electrons and protons; however, they may possess a varying number of neutrons. The atoms of a given element that possess a different number of neutrons are the isotopes of that particular element. They occupy the same place in the periodic table and exhibit typically similar chemical behaviour.

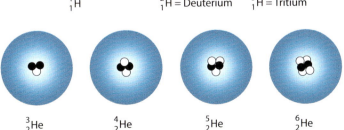

Isotopes of hydrogen and helium.

SCIENCE ENCYCLOPEDIA

Chemical Bonds

A chemical reaction refers to the making and breaking of chemical bonds. In order to understand a chemical reaction, we must understand what bonds are. The strength of a bond denotes the difficulty to break a bond. The length of a bond indicates the structural information and the positions of the atomic nuclei. "Bond dipoles" reveal the electron distribution around the two bonded atoms. From bond dipoles, we can derive electronegativity data that is useful for calculating the bond dipoles of bonds that may have never been made before.

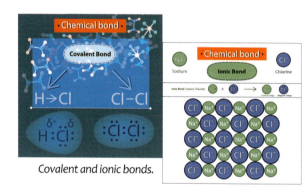

Covalent and ionic bonds.

Types of bonds

There are two fundamental types of bonds: covalent and ionic. In a covalent bond, an equal sharing of the electrons between the nuclei of atoms occurs. Covalent bonds are formed between atoms of approximately equal electronegativity (tendency to attract electrons). As each atom has a near equal pull for the electrons in the bond, the electrons are not completely transferred from one atom to another.

Forming of anion and cation

Charles-Augustin de Coulomb

When the difference in electronegativity between two atoms in a bond is large, the more electronegative atom can strip an electron off of the less electronegative atom to form a negatively charged anion and a positively charged cation. The two ions are held together in an ionic bond because the oppositely charged ions attract each other, as described by Coulomb's Law.

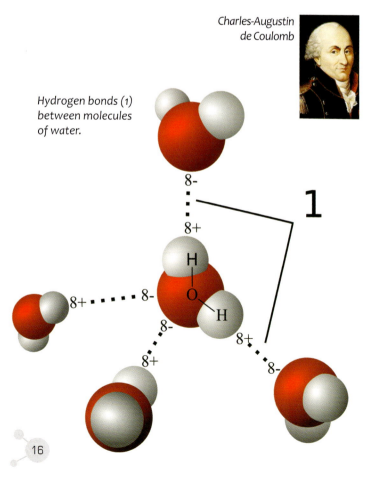

Hydrogen bonds (1) between molecules of water.

Bonding of atoms

In nature, some elements such as helium (He), neon (Ne) and argon (Ar) never bind to other atoms. Such elements are called noble gases. How are noble gases different from other elements? The answer lies in their closed shell electron configurations. Because the valence shell of a noble gas is completely full, it cannot accept another electron into the shell. The nucleus pulls the electron when it is positively charged. Therefore, the loss of an electron from a noble gas is critical. This is why noble gases are unreactive as they have filled valence shells.

Structure of xenon tetraflouride, one of the first noble gas compounds to be discovered.

THE PERIODIC TABLE

The first ever element was discovered by a man named Hennig Brand in 1649. He had discovered phosphorous. Within the following two centuries, many other scientists discovered and expanded the knowledge base on various other elements. By 1869, a total of 63 elements were discovered by various scientists around the world.

With each new discovery, scientists realised that the elements fell under a certain pattern. The periodic table was born from a desire to list and explain each of the discovered elements as well as to relate them to these patterns. The father of the periodic table according to some is a German chemist named Lothar Meyer, while for others, it is a Russian chemist named Dmitri Mendeleev.

SCIENCE ENCYCLOPEDIA

The Periodic Table

The periodic table is one of the most powerful tools in the hands of chemists. It is a systematic tabular arrangement of all the 118 chemical elements currently known to humans in order of increasing atomic number, that is, the total number of protons present in the nucleus of the atom.

Structure of the table

The usual format of the table consists of a grid of elements represented in 18 columns (called groups) and seven rows (called rows) with a separate double row of elements below. The table can also be interpreted by breaking it up into four rectangular blocks: the s-block on the left, the p-block on the right, the d-block in the middle and the f-block below that.

Arrangement of elements

When chemical elements are slotted into the aforementioned arrangement, a recurring pattern called the "periodic law" is formed as per their properties. Because of this, elements in the same column usually display similar properties while elements in the same row display a predictable variation in certain properties. This is extremely useful for scientists because it allows predictions to be made about a certain element based on its position in relation to another element. For example, if we know the properties of carbon, we can also make certain estimates about the behaviour of silicon (which falls right below carbon in the table). Without this arrangement, an experimental approach to the knowledge we seek about the chemical elements would give us very little insight.

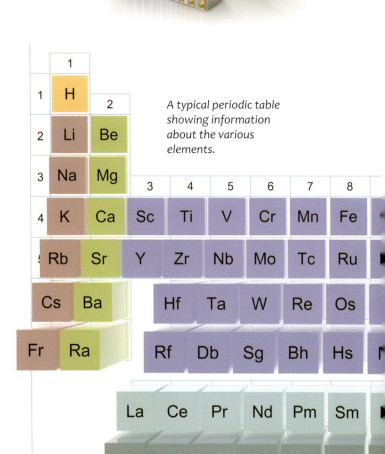

A typical periodic table showing information about the various elements.

Alkali metals

Alkali metals are the first group in the periodic table. This group includes lithium, potassium and the most commonly found alkali metal, sodium. These metals get their name because of their reaction with water, as a result of which they form alkaline solutions. However, metals such as caesium (Cs) and rubidium (Rb) have a volatile interaction with water. These metals are soft, white and are seldom found in their unadulterated form in nature.

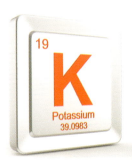

GENERAL SCIENCE

Beryllium is a steel-grey, lightweight and brittle alkaline-earth metal.

Alkaline-earth metals

Calcium, magnesium, barium and radium are all alkaline-earth metals that are found in compounds in Earth's crust. For example, beryllium (Be) is found in gemstones such as beryl and emeralds. Alkaline-earth metals react with water, although less violently than alkali metals and oxygen. Magnesium burns bright and has white ashes due to the presence of oxygen in the air. It is used to produce flares and fireworks.

FUN FACT
Despite the fact that they did not know each other, Dmitri Mendeleev and Lothar Meyer produced work that was remarkably similar in its research and presentation.

Transition metals

Transition metals consist a large group of elements which include the most common metals such as copper and chromium. Some of these elements have the ability to create a magnetic field, such as nickel and iron, and the densest, naturally occurring element, osmium (Os). With the exception of mercury, which is in the liquid state at room temperature, transition metals have high melting point. They are hard metals and their electrons are capable of flowing, making them good conductors of heat and electricity.

Poor and semi-metals

Metals that fall under this group are lead, tin, aluminium and bismuth. These metals are soft and have a lower melting point when compared to transition metals. These metals are extremely useful when mixed with another metals in an alloy. For example, bronze is made from an alloy of copper and tin. Semi-metals are those that have a few, but not all the properties of a metal; for example, arsenic (As), antimony (Sb) and boron (B).

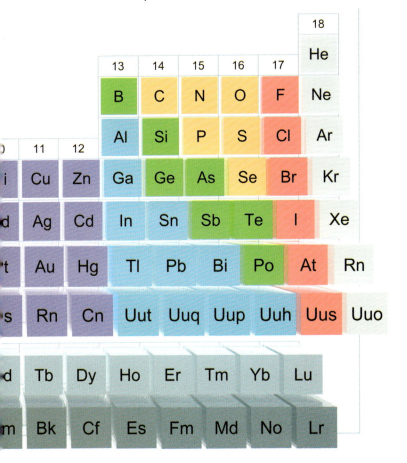

Noble gases

Noble gases are odourless, colourless and unreactive to a significant extent. However, it does not mean that they do not have any properties of note. They are useful gases. The second lightest gas after hydrogen is helium. Helium does not burn. This makes it safe to use in airships and in the tanks used by deep-sea divers. All noble gases (except helium) radiate light if electricity is passed through them. Therefore, they are used for lighting.

Non-metals

This refers to the common gases found in the atmosphere, such as oxygen, nitrogen and also carbon and sulphur (S). They are poor conductors of heat and electricity, and become fragile when in the solid state. There are certain non-metals called "halogens" that form salts with other elements such as chlorine.

Chlorine gas filled in glass container.

SCIENCE ENCYCLOPEDIA

History of the Periodic Table

Professor Dmitri Mendeleev, a Russian chemist, first published his periodic table in 1869. He then published an elaborated version in 1871. This version of the periodic table is generally regarded as the most influential and accurate one. Later, this was slightly reworked and extended by American chemist, Horace Groves Deming.

The monument honours Professor Dmitri Mendeleev. It shows his sculpture with the periodic table.

Telluric helix

In 1862, Alexandre-Emile Béguyer de Chancourtois, a French geologist, first published the basic and elementary form of the periodic table, which he called the "telluric helix". Here, the elements were arranged in a spiral on a cylinder in order of their increasing atomic weights. An English chemist named John Newlands wrote a series of papers from 1863 to 1866, where he found that when the elements were arranged in order of their increasing atomic weights, equivalent physical and similar chemical properties recurred at intervals of eight. He compared such periodicity to the octaves of music. This was called "the law of octaves".

Contributions by other scientists

Many chemists had tried their hand at classifying the elements before Mendeleev. In 1789, Antoine Lavoisier published a list of 33 chemical elements, arranging them into gases, metals, non-metals and earths. In 1817, Johann Wolfgang Dobereiner showed that the atomic weight of strontium lies midway between the weights of the elements calcium and barium. Some years later, he showed that other such "triads" exist. These are chlorine, bromine and iodine (halogens) and lithium, sodium and potassium (alkali metals).

Use in schools

Horace Groves Deming's 18 column table, first published in 1923, soon became standard study material in American schools. This was because a handout version of Deming's table was published by Merck and Company. Glenn T. Seaborg, an American chemist, won the Nobel Prize in 1951 as he had added the actinide block below the lanthanides. The award was also presented in recognition for his work on synthesising these elements.

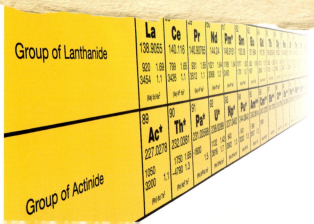

GENERAL SCIENCE

Periodic Trends

The great utility of the periodic table lies in how easily it makes predictions about the properties of a certain element based on its position with relation to some other element. Many chemical properties of elements show a certain periodicity.

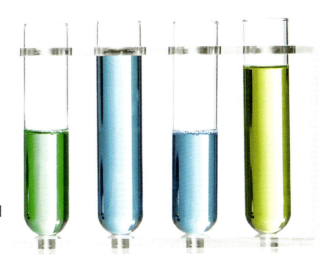

Electronegativity

Electronegativity is the measure of the tendency of an atom to attract electrons. An atom's electronegativity is affected by both, its atomic number and the distance between the valence (or outermost shell) electrons and nucleus. The higher the atomic number, the greater is the electrostatic attraction between an electron and a nucleus.

Ionisation energy

The ionisation energy of an element is the minimum energy required to displace a single electron from the outermost shell of an atom of that element in the gaseous state. It is dependent on the atomic number of the element and the size. Therefore, we see that ionisation energy increases along a period and decreases along a group. Some elements show slightly uncharacteristic ionisation energies.

Atomic radius increases

As we proceed down a group, the valence electrons will fill up higher electronic levels and the outermost shells spread further and further away from the nucleus. The intermediate electrons create a shielding or screening effect between the valence electrons and nucleus, thereby reducing the electrostatic interaction between them. Thus, these valence electrons are loosely held and the atomic radius, as a result, is large.

Atomic size decreases

Across a period, the atomic size gradually decreases. This is due to the fact that along a period, all the electrons are added to the same valence shell. However, simultaneously, the number of protons in the nucleus increases, making it more positively charged. The effect of the increasing atomic number outweighs that of the increasing electron number. Therefore, the nucleus attracts the electrons more strongly, drawing in the atom's valence shell closer to the nucleus.

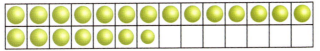

The figure schematically shows the atomic size of the elements in the periodic table.

SCIENCE ENCYCLOPEDIA

Valency

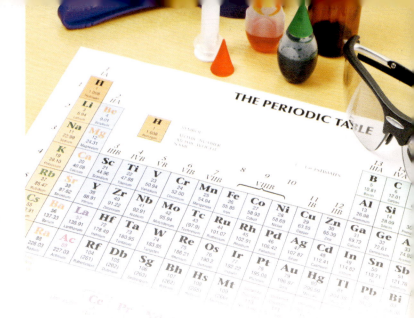

Valency is a property of an element that can estimate the number of other atoms with which the atom of the given element can bond with, simultaneously. Valence is at the very theoretical basis of the periodic table.

Theory of chemical valencies

The theory of chemical valencies may be traced back to an 1852 paper by Edward Frankland, where he used both theoretical and empirical evidence to demonstrate how atoms of certain elements would most likely bond with a given number of other atoms. Initially, the valency of an element was given by the number of univalent hydrogen atoms that it combined with.

Understanding valencies

The octet rule explains valency to a significant extent. According to this rule, all atoms aspire to the stable electronic configuration of the inert elements. Therefore, they either give away their valence electrons or bond with the requisite number of electrons to accommodate the difference. For example, elements in group one and 17 have valency one, elements in group 14 have valency four, those in group 15 have valency three and so on.

Facts about valency

In the periodic table, elements that are arranged in the same group have the same valency. The first group of elements has a valency of one, the second group has a valency of two, the third group has a valency of three and the fourth group has a valency of four. The fifth group in the periodic table has a valency of three, while the sixth group has a valency of two. The seventh group in the periodic table has a valency of one. However, the eighth group has a valency of zero.

FUN FACT

Frankland's discovery and study of the bond between atoms laid a foundation to modern day structural chemistry. He was eventually knighted for his work.

6 apples

2 apples shared

6 apples

The two children are like two atoms and the apples are like electrons. They create a bond by sharing two apples, so that each has 6+2=8 shared apples.

MATTER

Matter is any material that has inertia and occupies physical space. According to modern physics, it consists of various types of particles, each having its own mass and size.

Matter can exist in several states, which are also referred to as phases. The three states are solid, liquid and gas. When different kinds of matter come together, substances that may not resemble any of the original ingredients are formed. For example, hydrogen (a gaseous element) and oxygen (another gaseous element) combine to form water (a liquid element). This process is called a chemical reaction. A chemical reaction involves interactions between the electrons of the atoms, but does not affect the nuclei of the atoms. In some situations, atomic reactions convert matter into energy. This is known as a nuclear reaction.

SCIENCE ENCYCLOPEDIA

Definition of Matter

Matter is anything that occupies space and has mass. Matter is composed of atoms. Atoms are made up of subatomic particles called electrons, neutrons and protons. Neutrons and protons are the heaviest subatomic particles. They are clumped together in the centre of the atom and collectively form the nucleus.

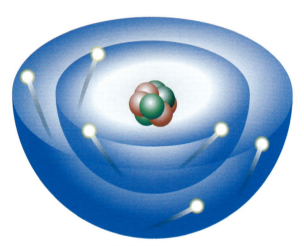

Inside of an atom.

What constitutes an atom?

Electrons, protons and neutrons together form atoms. There are more than 100 different types of atoms, each of which constitute a unique chemical element. Atoms combine to form a molecule. Atoms and/or molecules combine to form a compound.

Atoms are empty

The nucleus is surrounded by a cloud of electrons that are lighter than protons and electrons. More than 99 per cent of an atom is empty. Furthermore, atoms are composed of point particles that have no effective size or volume. These particles are called quarks and leptons. In an informal sense, matter refers to all physical objects. In a formal sense, matter could be defined as anything that has mass and volume.

Wolfgang Pauli, the scientist who proposed the Pauli Exclusion Principle.

For example, a pen is considered as matter because it has mass and occupies space. The simple observation that "matter occupies space" was made several decades ago, however its explanation is more recent. The explanation is believed to be the result of Pauli's Exclusion Principle.

GENERAL SCIENCE

Phases of Matter and Phase Diagram

Phases of matter refer to the regions where the physical properties of a material are essentially uniform. These physical properties primarily include state, density, mobility, refraction index and magnetisation among others. In the classical sense, matter basically has three phases: solid, liquid and gas. These phases are also referred to as states of matter. Besides solid, liquid and gas, there are other states such as plasma and more theoretical states such as the Bose–Einstein condensates and fermionic condensates. When considering the more fundamental particles, we get more states or phases like the quark–gluon plasma.

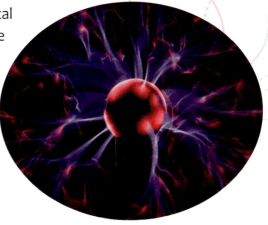

Plasma is one of the four fundamental states of matter, the others being solid, liquid and gas. Plasma has properties unlike those of the other states.

Inspection of water triple point cell.

Pressure and temperature

The state or phase of matter depends mainly upon pressure and temperature. Water is solid below 0° C under normal atmospheric pressure, but if the pressure is adequately low, it can melt below 0° C. In addition, water can be made to boil at a temperature higher than 100° C if the super incumbent pressure is adequately high. The phase diagram for a particular kind of matter is made by analysing its states under different pressure and temperature values. At a certain temperature and pressure, a certain kind of matter can exist in all three states. That point in the phase diagram is called triple point. For water, it is 0.01° C in the temperature axis and 6.1173 millibars in the pressure axis.

Effect of pressure

It is important to note that at a pressure other than the atmospheric pressure, the phase stability region would also change. Therefore, it is possible to keep water in the liquid state even at a temperature higher than 100° C by maintaining the pressure.

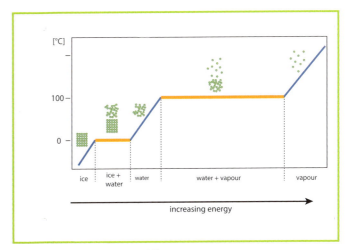

Phase stability of water at different temperatures.

SCIENCE ENCYCLOPEDIA

States of Matter

Solid, liquid and gas are the three states of matter. We find materials in these states of matter every day. The existence of matter in a particular phase depends on the kind of temperature and pressure it is exposed to. Temperature is simply the measure of how hot or cold a substance is.

Molecular changes

All molecules of matter have a vibrating motion. When their temperature is raised or heat is supplied, the molecules get more energy and vibrate more vigorously. Once the molecules overcome intermolecular attraction, also called van der Waals force, as well as the pressure they are exposed to, they start to separate from one another, thus resulting in a phase change.

Geckos can stick to walls and ceilings because of van der Waals forces.

States of matter

Solids
The atoms and molecules of a solid are tightly packed together in a regular arrangement. The particles in a solid continue moving, but their movement results in a minor vibration. Therefore, they have a definite shape; for example, a round ball and a square book. Solids have a definite volume and a fixed shape.

Liquids
The molecules of a liquid are very close to each other and can also slip over each other to change their position. Liquids have a definite volume but they do not have a definite shape. Liquids can be pushed through a tube, but they cannot be compacted to fit into a limited space. They can move and take the shape of the vessel that they are in. Viscosity determines how easily liquids flow. Liquids that have high viscosity (such as honey) do not flow freely.

Gases
The molecules of a gas are not close to each other, and can move easily and quickly. Therefore, gases can expand to fill a vessel. Gases have a low density. They do not have a fixed shape or volume and thus they can be condensed, reducing the space between their particles. Most gases are invisible. Steam rising from a hot bowl of soup is only visible once it begins condensing and forms a vapour of water droplets.

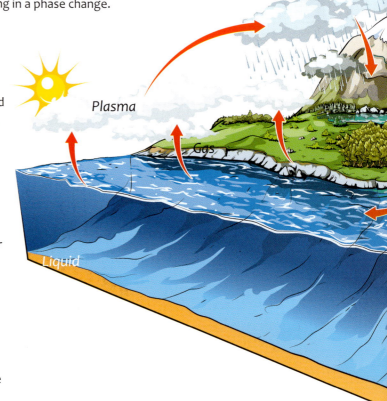

Plasma
There is a fourth state of matter called plasma. It is found throughout the universe but seldom on Earth. It is caused when radiation or very high temperatures pull electrons away from atoms. It exists in a gas-like state. This creates a gaseous cloud of positive ions and negative electrons. It is a good conductor of heat and electricity, and is found around the Sun. In natural light, it appears in the sky in the form of an aurora.

GENERAL SCIENCE

Transformation of matter

When matter melts
When matter melts, it changes its state from solid to liquid. This phenomenon occurs when the temperature is increased, causing the particles in a solid to vibrate rapidly. The temperature at which this occurs is called the melting point of the solid. Tungsten, a metal, has the highest melting point among metals, which is 3420° C.

Evaporation
Evaporation is the process in which a liquid changes into a gas. Evaporation occurs when molecules in the liquid's surface have sufficient energy to move away from each other and thus form a gas. For example, water on the road evaporates as water vapour into the atmosphere. In addition, liquids evaporate rapidly when heated. This is seen when water is kept to boil.

Condensation
Condensation is the process by which a gas on cooling turns back into a liquid. When gas molecules lose heat and energy they slow down. They move closer and form a liquid. An example of condensation is when water droplets form on the outside of a glass of cold water.

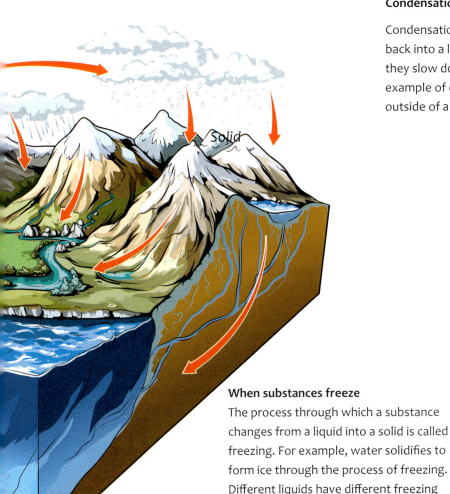

Illustration showing the states and transformation of matter.

When substances freeze
The process through which a substance changes from a liquid into a solid is called freezing. For example, water solidifies to form ice through the process of freezing. Different liquids have different freezing points, that is, the point below which they will transform into a solid. Water has a freezing point of around 0° C whereas mercury freezes at –38° C.

> **FUN FACT**
> *There is a stark difference between the predicted rotations of the galaxy about its centre and the observed values. This difference is said to be the effect of dark matter.*

Dark matter

The rest of the universe consists of dark matter and dark energy. Dark matter is studied more in astrophysics and cosmology than in physical science. Dark matter cannot be perceived; neither does it give out any sort of electromagnetic radiation nor does it reflect any back. However, like all matter, its presence affects the gravitational fields and hence, its effects can be seen as those of gravitational forces on visible objects. An example would be the rotation of the Milky Way itself.

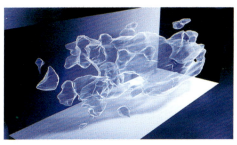

3D map of the large-scale distribution of dark matter, reconstructed from measurements of weak gravitational lensing with the Hubble Space Telescope.

SCIENCE ENCYCLOPEDIA

Properties of Matter

All substances have a varied array of different characteristics called properties. The property of a substance denotes its features or qualities, right from its appearance to its chemical or physical attributes. Scientists and engineers use the information on the properties of various substances to choose an appropriate material for particular applications in industries and in research.

A diamond has a hardness rating of 10 on the Mohs scale of mineral hardness.

Hardness

This property determines how easy or difficult it is to shape or scratch a substance. A common method to measure the relative hardness of a substance is to use the Mohs scale. Ten minerals ranging from the hardest to the softest have been ranked on the scale. A substance's ability to resist getting scratched by another substance determines its hardness on the Mohs scale.

Conduction of electricity

Materials that are good electric conductors enable an electric current to pass through them with ease. Metals are good conductors of electricity. Copper is used to make electrical wires. Materials such as plastic, ceramics and glass are poor conductors of electricity. They are used as insulators that prevent electricity flow to places where it is not required.

Copper wires (good conductor of electricity) covered by plastic (bad conductor of electricity).

Solubility

Solubility refers to the ability of a substance to dissolve in water. Some materials can dissolve in water or any other liquid to form a mixture. Water is often referred to as the universal solvent as most substances can dissolve in it.

Flexibility and elasticity

Flexibility refers to the ability of some materials to twist or bend, whereas elasticity refers to the ability of a material to absorb force as well as twist or stretch in different directions before returning to its original position. Interestingly, some materials have a limit to their elasticity. If they are stretched beyond their normal tolerance, they will not return to their original shape and size.

Mass and density

Density refers to the weight of a substance in relation to its size. To find the density of a material, divide its mass by its volume. Dense materials such as brass and lead are used for weights, whereas materials with low density (such as wood) float on water. Air-filled foam pellets have extremely low density and, therefore, are used to protect electronic goods and other fragile materials.

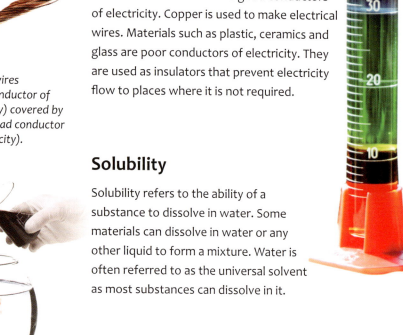

A graduated cylinder containing various coloured liquids with different densities.

28

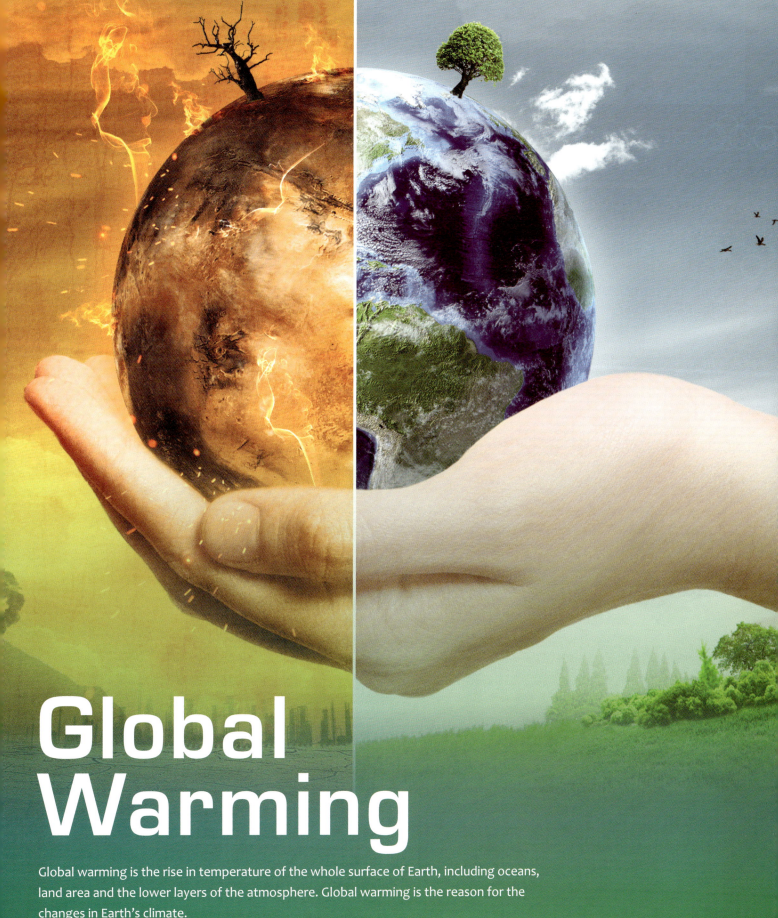

Global Warming

Global warming is the rise in temperature of the whole surface of Earth, including oceans, land area and the lower layers of the atmosphere. Global warming is the reason for the changes in Earth's climate.

The debate regarding the existence of global warming is continuously going on. Scientists have proven by many facts that the temperature of Earth has risen approximately 0.4–0.8 in the past 100 years. A major part of the heat absorbed by Earth goes into oceans, which causes the ice on the Polar regions to melt. This has created confusion among scientists when they attempt measuring global warming.

SCIENCE ENCYCLOPEDIA

Greenhouse Effect and Greenhouse Gases

The lower layer of the atmosphere that is getting warmer is an extremely thin layer. Many greenhouse gases are found in this layer that possess the capacity to capture heat. Thus, these gases ultimately warm the surface of Earth. This process of absorption and emission of heat by the gases is called the greenhouse effect.

Carbon dioxide, CFCs, ozone, methane, nitrous oxides and water vapour are commonly considered to be greenhouse gases. A balanced amount of these gases prevents our planet from becoming too hot or too cold. Water vapour is a naturally occurring greenhouse gas, which balances its quantity on its own.

In recent years, many human activities have contributed to increasing the quantity of these gases tremendously. These are burning fossil fuels, coal, petroleum, oil, deforestation, and increasing use of land for agriculture and building purposes.

The percentage of carbon dioxide has increased approximately 100 ppm in just a few years. CO_2 is the gas that can remain in the atmosphere for a very long period of time and have adverse effects on the atmosphere.

Gases and water vapour rise into the atmosphere and trap all the heat released by the Sun.

Effects

Recent studies have shown that drought, climate changes and earthquakes are also the result of global warming. There are many impacts of global warming on our environment as listed below:

1. Rising level of oceans
2. Changes in rainfall quantity and pattern
3. Occurrence of events like flooding, droughts and hurricanes
4. Melting of the glaciers and ice at the poles
5. Extinction of species
6. Widespread of endemic diseases
7. Damage to the ocean ecosystem causing the coral reefs and planktons to vanish
8. Acidification of the ocean water

Global warming can result in changes in the ecosystems, causing some species to move farther north and evolve and multiply, while others won't be able to move and might become extinct. This will upset the balance of nature and cause repercussions beyond comprehension.

Solutions

Carbon sequestration, mitigation and adaptations can be looked at as possible solutions.

Mitigation

These are the combinations of activities for reducing the emission of greenhouse gases and formation of carbon sinks. Energy conservation, increasing energy efficiency and use of low-carbon energy technologies like renewable energy, nuclear energy and carbon capture can prevent global warming. There are basic things that can be done at home. Turning off the fans, lights and all the electronics in the house when not in use could contribute to the environment. Unplug electronics that can be unplugged. Avoid the use of air conditioners and deodorants that have CFC in them as they contribute to global warming.

Carbon sequestration

Carbon sequestration is the technique of capturing carbon by different ways like increasing plankton growth in the oceans or draining the released carbon dioxide into oil wells. This method has not yet been implemented.

The effect of global warming on the water bodies of Earth.

GENERAL SCIENCE

Arresting Global Warming

If we study the seriousness of global warming, it can be very daunting. There is no single solution to it but by carrying out a few steps, we can control global warming. Every individual can play a role in controlling this problem.

Stopping the emission of greenhouse gases today will not immediately bring down the temperature; however, it would definitely make a difference in the long-term.

Solutions

Reduction in emissions

IPCC has declared that we have to reduce the emissions of greenhouse gases by 50–80 per cent to attain the required harmless concentration. As an individual, we can do this on a personal level, as well as encourage the government to take some steps in this direction.

The gases released from industries, vehicles and power plants should be analysed properly before being released into the air. In addition, the vehicles used should be properly maintained and inflated. Air travel contributes more to global warming than any other means of transport, so travel less by air.

Stop deforestation and promote plantation

We can control up to 20 per cent of the emissions from reaching the atmosphere by stopping deforestation. As forests can absorb large quantity of emissions, they act as natural sequesters. Growing more and more plants, recycling paper, buying used furniture and goods, using improved agricultural practices, and forest management are some practices that we should adapt compulsorily. We should not waste paper and make use of cloth instead of paper tissues. These practices can take care of a major chunk of the existing emissions.

Promote plantation.

Boosting energy efficiency

Energy is primarily used in power generation and for heating and cooling spaces. With some adjustments in our way of living, we can control the emission of many pounds of carbon dioxide into the atmosphere.

Some of these ways are:

- Use CFLs or LEDs lighting
- Use thermostats
- Electrical appliances with more energy stars should be purchased
- Regularly clean the filters in air conditioners and furnaces, and defrost the freezer.
- Electrical appliances should not be left on standby mode.
- Refrigerators and freezers should not be kept near furnaces, dishwashers or boilers as they end up consuming more power.

FUN FACT

The Arctic, which is already the fastest warming part of the planet, will see temperatures rise by 1.1 °F per decade by 2040.

SCIENCE ENCYCLOPEDIA

Mass bike ride in Thailand to reduce fuel consumption and global warming.

Recycled products.

- Replace air conditioners, fridges and furnaces that have been used for more than 4–5 years with new ones as they consume more power and give out more emissions after a certain period of time.
- The house should be properly insulated for maintaining the temperature and to lessen the burden on the heater and the cooler.
- Avoid using hot water for washing clothes and utensils.
- Use sunlight to dry clothes instead of using dryer every time.

Green transportation; public transport

Drive less and walk more. Plan car pooling or use public transport for travelling instead of using your own vehicle. Electric, smart cars and cars that run on vegetable oil or some other renewable source of energy. Their use should be encouraged. Use a bicycle instead of a car; it is not only healthy for the body but also for the environment. Additionally, you will save money on fuel.

Use of renewable sources of energy

We can use solar energy for cooking, heating and power supply. Currently, energy can be produced by the Sun, wind and burning biomass. The shift towards the use of renewable sources of energy can save money and reduce the emission of harmful gases too.

Conserve water

It requires a lot of power to draw water to the tanks and purify it. So, by conserving water, we can save energy as well.

Adaptation of zero carbon or low carbon technologies

With the advancement in science, many technologies using zero or very less carbon have come into existence. They should be used more frequently.

Eat more local food

Eat natural food instead of processed and packed foods. Eat vegetables and fruits that are grown in your locality instead of imported ones as a lot of fuel gets used in the production, packaging and transportation of food that is grown far away from you.

Reduce, reuse and recycle

We should not buy things unnecessarily and if needed, buy eco-friendly products. Always try to reuse your resources instead of buying new products with the same function. Recycle paper, bottles, glass, steel, aluminium foils, etc.

Spread awareness

The information provided to people for controlling global warming is often misleading. They should be properly guided as to how and what measures should be adapted to control global warming. Be a part of a global warming community and make yourself aware of many facts and solutions related to it.

Be prepared for the impacts

There are some consequences of global warming that are inevitable, like the sea level rising, extreme temperatures, growing wildfires and severe heat waves. Thus, we should be prepared for them. By adapting some simple changes in our daily life, we can reduce our carbon footprint and can give our future generation a better planet.